Vertigo
of
Risk

Selected works by Margaret Randall

Poems:
Stormclouds Like Unkept Promises
Out of Violence into Poetry
Starfish on a Beach: The Pandemic Poems
Time's Language: Selected Poems: 1959-2018
As If the Empty Chair / Como si la silla vacía
The Rhizome as a Field of Broken Bones
About Little Charlie Lindbergh
She Becomes Time
The Morning After: Poems & Prose in a Post-Truth World

Nonfiction:
Artists in My Life
Thinking about Thinking
I Never Left Home: Poet, Feminist, Revolutionary
My Life in 100 Objects
Che on My Mind
More Than Things
Haydée Santamaría: She Led by Transgression
Exporting Revolution: Cuba's Global Solidarity

Vertigo
of
Risk

poems

Margaret
Randall

Casa Urraca Press
ABIQUIU

Cover photograph by Margaret Randall.
Author photograph by Magdalena Lily McCarson.
Set in Nobel and Odile.

26 25 24 23   1 2 3 4 5 6 7

First edition

ISBN 978-1-956375-13-8

CASA URRACA PRESS

an imprint of Casa Urraca, Ltd.
PO Box 1119
Abiquiu, New Mexico 87510
casaurracapress.com

For Barbara,
always for Barbara.

Contents

"You've got to jump off cliffs all the time and build your wings on the way down."

—*Annie Dillard*

"Be ready at any moment to give up what you are for what you might become."

—*W. E. B. DuBois*

"I have come to believe over and over again that what is most important to me must be spoken, made verbal and shared, even at the risk of having it bruised or misunderstood."

—*Audre Lorde*

DEAREST

Dearest Ruth

Dearest Ruth, thank you for coming
if only in my dream.
Your visit surprised me
after the awkwardness between us
last time we spoke.

Of course, I knew you were raging,
confined as they had you,
longing for the Lakewood Avenue house
and your morning walks
around Fresh Pond.

You asked if I'd read your piece on Proust.
I said yes.
You asked what I thought
and I told you it's not finished,
you need to end with a warning, I said,

about consumer capitalism, use Hillary
as an example.
And then wondered
why I ever thought
I should give you advice.

Your addiction to a great man
surely allowed you
to understand the writer
who needed seven books
to explore the psychology of memory.

In my dream you reminded me
our memory was born
in that country where we met,
that country like a broken body now,
struggling to breathe.

Loving you as I did, I'm glad
you didn't live
to see it all come undone,
the questions we nurtured
disappearing on eroding shores.

But why Proust? Why not
some obscure
fourteenth-century woman alone in her lab,
reading another woman
in fading light?

Ruth Hubbard, 1924-2016

Dearest Mark

Dearest Mark, are we still on speaking terms
after that phone call echoing through time?
A stranger's voice pronouncing words I tried to erase
before they could take up residence in my ears.

Your giant heart exploding like calcium and rain,
tales of childhood in the bush
where rhinos challenged a queer storyline
and the road to your future stumbled.

Years, and I'm still angry you left so abruptly.
Not angry at you but at a world
where death devours without warning
and we are abandoned to the silence of suspense.

Zeus-like body preened and groomed,
feet that ran double marathons
on the blood-soaked earth of your first home
and the convoluted byways of your second.

It isn't your body, but your mind: unfinished novel
and arguments that hold me in close embrace,
fingers braiding and unbraiding memory
through narrow crevices of shame.

In pain you combed those rebellious strands
matted with their slime of lies,
nurtured each to a rebirth banished by many,
understood by those willing to risk fictitious comfort.

You showed me love of oneself leaves space
for the presence of friends if they can listen
to their own truth. I hesitated, then said yes
and never looked back except in this vastness
        of wanting.

Mark Behr, 1963–2015

Dearest Raquel

Dearest Raquel, when they die
in our dreams those we love
do so differently.
Emotion and the order of things:
shock or surprise may grab us
in slow motion or explode,
leaving our heartbeat erratic
for days to come.

It felt like news when an echoing voice
told me you were dead.
I found myself mentally calculating
your age, wondering if you were
younger or older than me,
then remembered
you died a decade ago.

Born in 1927, you left us in 2011:
my age now. Known as
la mariposa tallada en fierro,
the butterfly wrought in iron
or forged as a weapon
although you would have rejected
such imagery of war.

In my dream you were dying again
leaving me to ask
if one can repeat the process
just as we know we are born again
each time we fall in love, give birth,
write a successful poem or
make something new.

Don't worry. I will go to your words
for my answer, calm
my racing heart with the wisdom
you left in your time on earth.
You have done your living
and dying, have no more
mountains to climb.

Raquel Jodorowsky, 1927–2011

Dearest Claribel

Dearest Claribel, you of two homelands
and a lover from the ominous North,
the poems you wrote played in those spaces
you chiseled from pure grit.

Their words slept in your gracious smile
only to leap out and grab the traveler
by surprise. When your man died
he took his love and buried it

beneath a tree in your garden where a friend
caught sight of him sitting one day,
relaxed, at home, and as peaceful
as when he was alive.

You still yearned for him. All those
unfinished projects and the space
you made your own. Children remained
but went their own ways as you aged alone.

On our last visit I watched you accept
a hand-loomed tablecloth with a line
you'd written embroidered, white on white:
a gift from women you inspired far away.

You took the present with ladylike grace,
held it up for all to see, then gathered
the pure cotton and doubled it once more,
your secrets well-hidden between its folds.

Claribel Alegría, 1924-2018

Dearest Hilda

Dearest Hilda, you never said a word about
the cancer, even to family or friends,
your face growing thinner, pale
beneath that beehive of painted curls
and economist's mind.

Better known for your husband,
he of Don Quixote fame,
after he left you were judged
by patriarchal protocol, a lens
that rendered you invisible.

I remember our meeting in Mexico,
those fierce days of rebellion
and repression
destined to do us in.
You predicted as much.

And when we coincided in Lima
another fateful October,
El Cristo Morado blocking our attempt
to cross that city
of stubborn tradition.

Rarely Hilda Gadea, always *la primera esposa
del Che*, until you told your story
and even then, few acknowledged
you brought him into the fold,
made him the hero he would become.

I want to believe you will have a second chance,
another time in which to speak and act
on your own behalf
and without so much as a murmur
of denial.

Hilda Gadea, 1925-1974

Dearest Laurette

Dearest Laurette, more than friend
you were mother and sister,
the chosen kind:
diminutive body, painful history,
playful intuitive mind.

It was that intuition the experts
in your field couldn't abide,
attacking you as woman and foreigner,
ignoring or disqualifying
what you heard in your head.

Transporting yourself in space
and time, you understood
human sacrifice unfiltered
by the cultural judgements of today,
standing outside our calendar.

Ghosts of other wars.
Ghosts of another war.
Other ghosts of war.
This or that ghost. This war now.
Always one more war.

Delicate gloved hands on the steering wheel
of your gray Peugeot,
wicker basket with roast chicken,
French bread and patés.
Our picnics at Teotihuacan.

War and ghost trains. A child lost
on a railway platform,
fascism beneath your fingernails
threatening
the freedom in your hair.

You married great men
but were never
consumed by them.
Your love affair with Quetzalcoatl
defied the elements.

You brought mystery to
dialectical materialism,
crosshairs that would
come into focus in a future
you didn't live to see.

I didn't understand half
of what you said
but your words charged my memory,
illuminated my growing,
shaped who I would become.

When your daughter confided
she'd stopped you
from ending your life
I was speechless with rage
and grief.

From you I learned that creative women
become their own ghosts,
will always be spurned
and must die to be heard,
accepted, recognized.

Laurette Sejourné, 1911-2003

Dearest Felipe

Dearest Felipe, you were a man
large in art, grand gesture
entering a room, sucking
the air. We could only breathe
if we inhaled you.
I loved you despite yourself.

You produced beautiful children,
made new things,
exhibited a woman
whose creative brilliance shone
only after escaping
your furious orbit.

You married another goddess
but I doubt you stopped
bedding every woman who took
your fancy, that transgression
refined by the male
of our species.

I can imagine how vigorously
you fought the cancer
that took you, how you must have
brainwashed, bargained, bludgeoned,
hustled, coerced, and beaten it silly
in the night.

In death the edges of your body
seemed to push against
the confines of a coffin
that tried to contain your spirit
and your flesh. No use.
You won, if only by default.

Felipe Ehrenberg, 1943-2017

Dearest Roque

Dearest Roque, you were never content
to record your life as it was,
reinvented yourself many times over,
disguising cartwheels in every line.

Supplanting an absent father, you claimed
ancestry from the Dalton gang,
adding America's Wild West to your legacy,
spirited horses running in your dreams.

Jesuit studies sent you over to the other side
and you joined your tiny country's
Communist party, age fourteen,
Little Boy Lost at weekly meetings.

There was your escape from the clutches
of the CIA when an earthquake split
the walls of your prison and you disappeared
into a religious procession passing by.

It's time you tell me which stories were true
and which you imagined as your script
passing from mouth to mouth
after you were gone.

Your philandering was legion but so was
your generosity and your mind. I like to
imagine the words you left in a woman's voice
were inspired by our debates.

I still hear you explaining what Vallejo meant
as you helped me birth the hardest crossover
of my life: age to reason,
meaning to the newness of sound.

When you went home to fight for freedom
in El Salvador, no one could have known
your own comrades would torture and kill you:
brutal volley to an ambushed heart.

Now every May 10th your almost forty years
sink their teeth into wounds
that will not heal in my flesh:
too often betrayed, forever ready.

Roque Dalton, 1935-1975

Dearest Maru

Dearest Maru, in your family the men
became princes of industry,
the women expected to marry
moneyed businessmen.
Your mother lived her best life
a president's concubine.

You were a sheep of a different color
or, rather, no sheep at all.
In Tai Chi grace
brightly embroidered shifts
hid your communist commitment
and fiercest courage.

I brought my infant son to Mexico
and you took us in hand.
We met when you taught him
third-grade English. Together
we fought every crude assault
and trickster's slight.

I move through memory and see us
hiding in your home,
repression of 1969.
My partner at the time, our four
small children and I
all gathered before a black and white TV

that July 20th, balancing dinner
on folding trays, we
watched a man step onto the moon.
Your husband fearing
our presence would bring trouble
and you defying his fear.

Soon after, you left that relationship,
spent the rest of your life alone
rather than cater to men
who would try to mold you
to their pleasure
and despair.

By the time you called to say goodbye,
our years of resistance,
lives of our making
had stretched to take others in.
We'd done enough
to make each other proud.

I asked if you were in pain.
No, you said, though
your words were worn velvet,
see-through and very soft.
The cancer had already won.
Two days later you were gone.

So much we shared never found
its way into complete sentences
but continues to burn:
dead embers in your eyes,
still glowing ones
waiting their turn in mine.

Maru Uhthoff, 1937–2017

Dearest Michael

Dearest Michael, do you remember that afternoon
on the Great Lake of Nicaragua,
our tiny wooden boat bobbing on the surface
of impending war?

We talked about what we could do, how we
might help fix troubled waters,
if it's possible as outsiders to trade places
with those gone too soon.

I didn't know in a few short years I would
be calling you, asking your help
to fight a government that claimed
my work was "against the good order

and happiness" etc. etc., shallow definitions,
walls that keep people in or out
according to laws made by the bloodthirsty
to strangle the questioners.

You didn't hesitate before saying yes, rallied
an army in my defense and made sure
there was bread but roses too.
It was what you did.

You won many such battles, brilliant
jurisprudence and creativity
in your arsenal. But when it came
to your own private war

you couldn't achieve victory. The enemy
came wearing different clothes,
speaking in an unknown tongue:
insidious, implacable.

I think of you often: good man and experienced,
who turned family money to shelter
for those in need, once hid a rebel commander
months in your New York townhouse,

ran marathons of endurance, the ones for sport
and also those at the heart of what
true lawyering means:
that place where heart and history meet.

Michael Ratner, 1943-2016

Dearest Paul

Dearest Paul, it was hard to die
back when death
didn't enjoy its current range of action:
grabbed people right and left,
carried them off without warning.

They tell me you raged against
the cancer and I know
it must have been a struggle.
You had so much yet to dream,
to write, to do.

Translation wasn't common practice
when you brought Provençal
into English, surprised us
with Cortázar's *cronopios* and *famas*,
played games

with our minds beyond those poems
of your own that showed us
the city we lived in new to ear and eye:
that little girl moving fast
on the A train.

"Give the child words, give him/
words," you wrote, "and
he will use them." Simple as that.
Given the gift, you knew
how to pass it on.

Later I learned of the pictures you took
when I wasn't aware,
mementos you brought from Mexico
to my son's father
that he could trace the boy's life.

When I walk the streets of any
strange city I think of you,
filled with an energy
you would not live to use,
precious gifts we will never receive.

Paul Blackburn, 1926-1971

Dearest Clarence

Dearest Clarence, we were young
and those who were different
hung together, hiding our otherness
from the popular kids.

You never spoke of childhood pain,
a father who wanted you
to be a man or mother who loved
a son she didn't understand.

I didn't know your history, only
the kleptomania that grew
to embrace breaking and entering
as you got older.

Those were easier times and somehow
you always managed to avoid
the harsher punishments:
a criminal record or jail.

When you took a small Inca statue
from my shelf, I said nothing.
It was a reproduction
after all.

The next time I visited I slipped
a Navajo bracelet into my bag,
treasured its sandcast silver
and matrixed turquoise.

We traded back and forth after that,
never voicing the transgressions
but content our call and response
played tit for tat.

I ended up with the bracelet, can
barely remember the figurine,
our secret backs-and-forths standing in
for the words we couldn't speak.

They told me you died, and I thought
AIDS, but who knows? Many
of your friends had the Virgin of Guadalupe
tattooed on their backs.

You had her on your chest, a good way
to avoid getting hurt
by the rough trade you ran with
when you finally revealed yourself.

Clarence Huff, 1936-circa mid to late 1960s

Dearest Ceferino

Tough old guerrilla from the mountains
of Guerrero, member of
Genaro Vazquez's band,
fighting a nineteenth-century war
in twentieth-century Mexico.

Men on horseback with broken rifles
against a modern army,
no hope of victory,
vain faith giving you to believe
you had a chance.

Captured and imprisoned, you languished
for months until traded for
a Coca-Cola executive,
one kneecap putrid from the bullet
still lodged in your bone.

Cuba received you as it did so many,
hastening to heal
the pain of misadventure
and scars of unequal war,
turning grief to dignity.

We met in the hospital where they
tended your physical wounds,
managed to get you walking again,
but I saw something else in your eyes:
a longing for hot chile on your tongue.

Over dishes spiced with a local *picante*
you told me of crossing the border,
following the lettuce
in a land that exploited
then tossed you out.

When you spoke of your father, I asked
"How old is he?" "About my age,"
you responded, and continued to tell me
of your family, oblivious your answer
made no sense.

I don't know what became of you.
Perhaps you found your way
back to a familiar landscape
though surely not the place
that was rightfully yours.

Magic realism, real as your strong
hands and toothless smile,
like so many whose innocence
rebukes those forced
to deny their dreams.

Ceferino Contreras Ventura, 1917-1988

Dearest Anna

Anna Herrera wasn't your real name
but the one I remember, the one
I used in your honor, wrote under
when I needed to be
someone else.

Until you folded your body
over your infant daughter,
saving her life and forfeiting yours
as the car your husband drove
was hit by another,

you wrote brilliant feminist texts
as female consciousness spread
across your southern hemisphere
and others reached the place
you stood.

He remarried, couldn't tell your story
to the girl who never knew
her mother. But I still ask you questions,
hear your prescient answers
on the wind.

Anna Herrera was the name under which
Emma Herrera wrote and the one I later used
as a pseudonym in her honor. She was born
in 1942 and suffered an automobile accident
in 1973 that left her in a vegetative state.
She died in 1999.

Dearest Marv

Dearest Marv, the Army led you to
pacifism, your childhood rabbi
to the terrible knowledge
of how it feels
to be sexually abused by someone
who can do no wrong.

Yours was one of those lives
given to struggle,
little left for yourself.
You survived from the generosity
of those who honored the goodness
you bestowed upon the world.

When you needed a kidney transplant
a friend was quick to step forward
and offer his. Who knows
how long it might have added
to your life had it not been for one
small problem?

Who rejects such an offer out of
political difference? You did,
that's who, and you endured dialysis
so long as your body could
stand it. I remember
your raucous laugh,

the way your eyes sparkled when
you told some story
repeated often by a man
in love with justice, a repetition
forever welcome
because we loved you back.

Marv Davidov, 1931-2012

Dearest Phuc

Dearest Phuc, you knew how your name
sounded in English
and told us we could call you
Fernando,
but I always called you Phuc.

You chose me to teach you the language
of those who invaded
your precious land, said my accent
was common enough, like
that of the enemy.

Three times a week I knocked on your door,
sat across a heavy glass-topped table,
had you repeat verb forms
and pesky prepositions
until they sounded right.

You gave me stories in return: about
your family in Hanoi
escaping the bombs,
your wife who oversaw the anti-aircraft
artillery on your block.

Years later I happened to learn of your death,
long after the fact, and felt the pain
of not having known
like the projectiles that murdered
so many of those you loved.

Your gentleness lives in me still.
I'm proud to think
I could give you something:
simple friendship
between human beings.

Nguyen Phuc, 1930-1982

Dearest Paul

Boston, late 1980s, I was reading my poems, looked up
and saw you standing in the back, listening
with unbroken intensity. I could also see your friend
tugging your elbow and pointing at his watch.

You stood against the back wall to the end
and we talked briefly before he finally
dragged you off, explaining you had a plane
to catch. *Paul Farmer*, you said as you gestured
      goodbye.

I won't pretend we were friends. I saw you only
that once, corresponded some, then read
a biography introducing me to the doctor who traded
Harvard hospital for earthquake-torn Haiti.

Later I followed you 'round the world, to Rwanda
and other outlier countries where you
treated people with tuberculosis, Ebola, and AIDS,
each with its backstory of poverty and despair.

I would read about you walking miles to make sure
patients took their medicine, and remember
how you listened to my poems, insisted on staying
to the end at risk of missing your flight.

A focus as deep for words as for lives, unbroken
attention of a man who sees whole human
beings. Today I learn of your death at sixty-two,
sudden cardiac arrest in a village called Butaro

where you stopped much too soon, bequeathing
an example that challenges injustice,
a single man who took on the job
institutions and governments refuse.

Paul Farmer, 1959-2022

Dearest Kathy

Dearest Kathy, in a room with its furniture
bolted to the floor, prisoners and visitors
at cement tables, officer's eyes
forbidding us to touch.

No touching the vending machines either,
dehumanization the goal. I deposited
coins, bought paper cups of soup
and stale crackers wrapped in cellophane.

I also deposited memory in your hands,
as you in mine, knew you had
a life before, dreamed you might have one after.
Passionate talk. Passionate silences.

And you did have a life after those twenty-two years,
one you created from the friction
between control and hesitation, the unknown
bothering patience in your flesh.

Free, you rode your bike in Central Park,
worked tirelessly for those you left behind,
welcomed a grandchild to a world
where another opponent had you in its grip.

After struggles we cannot imagine, you left,
drying our tears on the way out,
one last conversation as you swallowed regret,
igniting. Igniting.

Kathy Boudin, 1943-2022

Dearest Ambrosio

Dearest Ambrosio, everyone
called you Pocho but me.
I preferred your given name
like the sweet nectar
of some rare flower,
delicate but fierce
against whatever storm.

Your keen mind sounded
when your country
needed it most, clarity
against repression,
courage against mediocrity,
a voice that didn't mind
standing alone.

I knew you as sentinel
but also neighbor,
the guy upstairs
who lent *Tin Tin* to my daughter
and always had time
to explore the depths
of a revolution in turmoil.

On recent visits to your
island under siege
an hour or two with you
calmed my fears,
helped me to contemplate
the big picture,
take the longer view.

Your gracious smile did its best
to hide your fragility,
hovered at its edges.
With your beloved Silvia
you are our neighbors still,
small of stature,
larger than life.

Ambrosio Fornet, 1932–2022

VERTIGO of RISK

Nepantla

In memory of Gloria Anzaldúa,
1942-2004.

The space between is not always a borderland,
division between nations, origins,
even such aspects of being no longer
one or the other
but histories slammed together by rape,
cowering in fear, surviving
through the brilliance and cunning
of beings set on opposing journeys
finding a compromise they didn't seek.

Napantla separates two bodies of water
and also the death-defying drops
on either side of that narrow ridge
we humans walk
on this journey called living.
As the word rose on our ancestors' tongues
it ceased to describe only heritage,
warring factions or that melting pot
that is never what it pretends.

Living between cultures, ages, ideas
that say yes, we see double,
grasp magnets pulling us this way
and that, embrace
all that has fed us to now.
We celebrate change
as we experience ourselves
swinging back and forth, steady beat
of momentum, creative passion on fire.

Some know it as no-man's land,
a strip of earth
to keep warring visions of life apart,
a place that doesn't exist on any map
or hum in any key heard by those
imprisoned by time.
Then flowers began to grow, birds sing
and animals inhabit what we abandon
in our shame.

Some are born understanding Nepantla
runs through our bodies
and tend both sides as if they are gardens
of Eden. We know it is up to us
to choose which side lives and which dies,
spend years learning to ask
those questions that will keep us safe,
answers that will bring us
closer to ourselves.

Each of us holds that liminal reality
within, memory whispers
many names, we take what we need
or maybe what we can get
when both sides retreat from the middle,
battle lines imposed by bullies who possess
the largest fortunes, best technology,
lightest skin and most devious minds
used in pursuit of conquest.

Crossroads? That place where paths diverge
and we believe we must choose
one direction or another.
No. Never so easy or mundane.
Nepantla is the world the artist fills
with imagination, that space where we take
our ancestry in hand, use what we need,
discard what is harmful or superfluous,
speak our names.

What they cannot know because it has fled
their courtyard, left the premises
of collective knowledge, is that we,
the vanquished, carry Nepantla in our flesh.
It is part of us, essence of how we feel
and move, where we go
taking that territory as a gift
to our children and children's children,
generations into a future we can only dream.

Nepantla is that place where multiple forms
of reality emerge simultaneously.
Sixteenth-century inhabitants
of Mexico's altiplano, invaded by the Spanish,
described an in-between
where they experienced slavery and resistance
moving through their veins,
call and response as old as the horror
humans inflict upon humans,

and new as tomorrow, gleaming as sun
on skin that has weathered
eons of land grabs, centuries of pain
suffered not in honor
but with the courage of a newborn
when she opens her eyes
and begins to learn
she will have to defend herself
against armies of entitlement.

The space between is not always a borderland
or even a puzzle's unfinished edge
crashing against another puzzle.
Nepantla is where we meet ourselves
when hope is dead
but tiny shoots of green emerge
from earth we must nourish with what we see
when we close our eyes
and reach back through history.

When I Lived

When I lived, I passed through a place
inhabited by ghosts.
If you slow your step
you can feel them hiding
in their fancy clothes among the trees.

My shadow remains in that place,
retreating midday
and stretching its lonely arms
in early morning and late afternoon
as it sings off-key to itself.

Those who find themselves there by chance
may feel my presence, the nudge
of my elbow or smoldering of my desire,
may hear the rustle of my words
caught in the highest branches.

But those who seek out that place
as destination
receive complete sentences, a music
beyond their imagination, a certainty
in the quickening of their pulse.

Danger shows itself in many disguises,
plays a rough game
and gives you to know that only risk
will take you where you want to go,
leaving your name as cairn.

Vertigo of Risk

Something in our breath reverberates,
spiraling from ancient grunts
and cries
born before words climbed into our throats
signaling the byways
leading us home.

Those paths are fraught with battles
neither of our making or choosing,
directional changes so brutal and unexpected
we may fall off the crater's rim
oblivious to the burning magma
churning below.

Our task is not only to acknowledge
the grunts but to invent
a new language able to define
and build, a vocabulary
that will reach the hearts of strategists
and neighbors.

We cling to hands held out in false support,
unaware their seductive grasp
pulls us closer to the edge,
take solace in words pronounced
by others who would lure us
to paralysis.

Reaching deep for those primordial sounds,
gathering and nurturing them
meaning by frightful meaning,
the vertigo of risk is always a danger.
Remember, almost anything is worth the chance,
and also note the word *almost*.

One Degree of Heat or Cold

A sudden gulp of air, slight change in
direction. You forget your keys
and must go back
to the house, open your door
a second time.

That return means you are there
when the telephone rings
or remind yourself you wanted to call
a friend you haven't seen
in years.

Casual moments, repeated or forgotten
in a day's routine, fade into
the comings and goings that hold time
in their solid grip and position
decision on your lips.

A speck of cosmic dust or wayward drop
of rain may start a war,
pull you into silence or send you
over the edge
of the nearest precipice.

One degree of heat or cold may place you
in danger's way or surround you
with love you couldn't imagine.
It is up to you to distinguish
and choose.

Geode

You need a hammer and strong hand
to split this lump of gray rock
hiding its crystal beauty, a world
where geology's heart takes you
into its wonder.

It is nature's piñata, shining star
deeper and more hidden
than that shower of candy and trinkets
giving way to the birthday child's
final blow.

I would crawl inside it if I could,
curl my body into its mystery:
roam its billions of years,
become one with the energy
of its desire.

Waving Goodbye to Roe v Wade

Written as a stacked Court
prepares to pound the
final nails in the coffin.

You devour us like pieces on a chessboard
riven by fault lines of fear,
neat squares frozen in your camouflage of hate.
You forget we are givers of life
and can erase you with our Lysistrata instinct
for making a home where all can live.

Rivers of rushing water clear as the sweetest song,
rocks descending mountainsides
to melt into earth, then rising again
in a language you've never learned to speak:
pure memory reflecting off the light
on ancient walls.

Were it not for your sad game, tricking us to your image,
poisoning us with your need for control,
values we will not mimic then or now or ever,
you would render us invisible, but we will not comply
even when life's pendulum
sweeps you from stage center.

The Aging Poet #1

The paper is always there
though no longer paper
but a computer's
backlit screen.

The pencil is ready, though
it's not a pencil
but your own arthritic fingers
moving across a keyboard.

Ideas explode from a forest
of synapses
firing slower than in youth
but with better aim.

Seven decades ago, my words stumbled
into pits of youthful hesitation:
dodged weeds pushing their way
through unyielding earth.

Today those words fly free.
They have learned
to navigate the earth's crust
and every smug impediment.

The Aging Poet #2

The nameless feeling
raised its hand.
It crouched and sprang,
rarely landing on its feet.

Words so often unable
to connect
with one another
fell broken about me.

Now, so much closer to the end
than where I started out,
those words inhabit
their strength.

Coming to a split in the road
they know which way
to go, how loud to shout
to be heard above

the confusion determined
to silence my rage,
absorb my energy,
deny the power of my voice.

The Aging Poet #3

For Raul Zurita.

No longer must I write
in male voice
or employ clues
only the choir knows.

I drag myself across the sky
in capital letters
that do not fade,
pulled by supersonic flight.

But I don't forget this freedom
is nurtured by the blood
of those who preceded me,
their courage and risk.

So much of what I am stands
upon the aching shoulders
of brave sisters
denied their birthright of truth.

Twilight

They call it the twilight of our years
as if muted pinks and golds
may produce one final show of light
streaking across dulled eyes.

I see bright colors, a sun powerful
enough to sustain life
on a planet where we threaten it
at every turn.

Like some aloof house cat, pity
crowds my space, wants to
take me by the hand and pull me
gently to the finish line.

But I am running my own race,
celebrating rebellion
along the way. My pace is passionate
as it breathes.

Your ministrations are obstacles
I must avoid. Your sympathy
lacks the agility
of divination.

Twilight is far too tame a horizon
to catch the glint in my eye,
amplify the words still assembling
on my lips.

Why not call it sunrise or dawn:
threshold to one last spurt
of imagination, the unimaginable
that brings us home?

Back to Front or Inside Out

Neither political nor pastoral
because the brushstroke
is broad, the paint
still wet and glistening.

Not a how-to manual because
the instructions can be read
in any order, back
to front or inside out.

No list or table of contents
with items to be added
or subtracted
according to whim, one by one.

Nor an outline with points
to be fleshed out
as sunrise extends
your line of sight.

The poem happens on its own
terms, no rules dragging
behind: the proverbial
tail between its legs.

It arrives upright, full-throated,
and you must get
out of its way,
let it take shape and shout.

Mother

She gave me life, purged me
from her body
into a world reduced
to her parameters
where I struggled against
her frustrations, fears, shame.

She visits rarely now, only
in dreams
or when I sit anxiously,
head in hands,
seeking that word or image
hiding in broad daylight.

I no longer remember her voice,
only those gestures
that betrayed the demeanor
she worked so hard to cultivate
through years battling
what was done to her.

I know she loved me.
She told me often
although the words sounded
brittle against the walls
of a compression chamber
made of broken glass.

It's been fifteen years since she left
and her image and scent
have faded but are part
of that great storm of *before*,
people and places
struggling for definition in my mouth.

Then, when I least expect her
she is here beside me
holding out her bony hand,
staring with unflinching eyes
and the immense courage
I never knew she had.

My Father's Eyes

As he left, his eyes led the way:
receding films, distant
and tired, sinking into an armature
of dying flesh.

My father was kind and gentle,
refusing to re-edit
his own progenitor's
cold disdain.

Dad saw good everywhere
and sang its chorus
though liberation never embraced him
while he lived.

As his eyes disappeared
into slowing eddies
I imagined them opening wide
on another shore,

spreading again to contain
a pulsing ocean
in a place where unquestioning love
would be his.

In a Name

What is absent from a name,
missing piece of the puzzle
and what remains
has us running in place
for centuries.

Shakespeare or Miles,
Cleopatra, Che,
Michelangelo
and the young girl
we call Mary

or BVM for short: Blessed
Virgin Mary
even knowing
the virgin designation
is poor translation

and the blessed was added
by those who came later,
adoring a symbol
to place on the other side
of this scale

we wield to separate
right from wrong,
good from bad,
submission to counter
temptation and fear.

Those known by first
or last alone
give us something
of ourselves, something
that wakes us forever.

Your Love of Here

For Sabra Moore and Roger Mignon.

Twenty acres of rugged land keep you
in a world apart, each view
carefully framed by kitchen windows
you designed: multicolor mesas,
trees in love with one another
hundreds of years, canyons
inscribed with the art of ancestors.

You came from your own artists' life
in a New York of bully landlords
and secret gardens
to discover this hollow you claimed
as home, every adobe laid by hand,
every corner of the house
shaped and painted by your creativity.

Digging the well, urging water
to the surface of parched earth,
decades of chopping and stacking wood,
the last nine loads traded
for a truck with 340,000 miles
of faithful service: your story
from prime to age.

Your spirits embedded in every beam
and brick sing a chorus of rapport
with the seasons, a rhythm that ties you
to the materiality of earth,
vastness of sky,
redtail hawk flying overhead
and mountain lion's haunting shadow.

Now you fight illness along with
the precarious economy
that's been your unfailing companion.
I watch one of you grow thin,
the other slowly make your way down
kitchen steps you once took in stride,
all things changing but your love of here.

We who care, worry about the years
to come, how you will manage
the demands of a home
that would challenge even the young.
Then I see the shadows of monsoon clouds
moving over rock, the imprint
of unfolding history in your eyes.

Your chickens keep on giving eggs,
woodstoves keep you warm,
the water level rises and falls
according to whim
and you are here, here for the duration,
unwilling to listen to anyone else's
skewed advice.

Fighting the Good Fight

For Bryce.

Inherited cancer collides with
your effort to swallow
and they embrace one another, dancing
to the edge of the picture plane.

You tell me your father and his brother
both died of this menace, a statement
matter of fact as it is brave, concise
as it fills all breathable air.

In my dream you look as you did
that day I handed you
my long-ago book, hoping you would
tell me you wanted to publish it.

And you did. It's been a dozen years
and more than a dozen books.
You aren't just publisher
but friend, curator of my poems,

of these words I put into our world
like arrows aiming deep
or rounding corners as they search
targets on a shifting horizon.

Now my words want only to hold
you close, embrace you
with strength and luck enough
to emerge on the other side.

Not that other side dressed in garments
of make-believe we invent
to give comfort when death appears
long before the finish line

but here and now where your
three-year-old Max
pretends to be a statue and
you keep on making books.

In my dream I cannot see
how the dance ends,
always wake too soon
or lose you to morning mist.

Somewhere beyond my sight line
I know you are fighting
the good fight and want to believe
you are winning.

Evolution of the Species

I have no use for your middle ground,
don't want your acquiescence
inclined neither right nor left,
not a clue to what you feel.

Your lies are pitiful as stale jokes
without punch lines,
stories where every piece
of the jigsaw fits.

Paper dolls with an outfit for every occasion
and packaged by color or style,
you lack the depth
that would let you breathe.

I'm unimpressed by your saccharine manner,
phrases cut from Hallmark verse
or answering-machine message
wishing me *a blessed day*.

An even temper is no temper. I'd rather
know the temperature at which
your blood begins to boil or ancestral bias
fossilized your pallid brain.

Don't give me that pat on the shoulder,
rictus smile or snippet
of tin laughter echoing on a day
too cold for any calendar.

Pretending it's all right doesn't make it
right, just adds a superfluous stripe
to the rainbow arching
across that pulsing sky.

When you say what you think, you risk
a response from me. Don't be afraid.
It's the give and take
called evolution of the species.

They Called Them Worms

When people emigrated
from Cuba in the 1970s and 1980s,
repudiation mobs gathered,
calling them gusanos *or worms.*

Humiliation's memory
is like the short fuse
on pyrotechnic promise,
spewed by those urged on
by bottomless doubt
or hunger for a fullness of self
they can't otherwise attain.

A bilious tongue believes
it can reduce its target
by invoking the lowliest
of creatures—*worms*—
oblivious that even worms
possess a dignity
above their own.

I have heard this weapon
wielded by cowards
blindly following leaders
who may not have spawned
such noxious sewage
but did nothing to overcome
its stench.

Its ugly memory accompanies me
and the shame lingers.
I didn't join the mob
but neither did I speak out
against its intolerance.
That failure still sickens
my every cell.

When they do not become
the change
they have been waiting for,
revolutions risk devolving
into what they fought:
a wound
that does not heal.

Perimeters

The chocolate lab pants at the bars
of her four-by-six cage
each time she senses an opportunity
for escape.

Meanwhile, your house cat
dozes calmly
allowing you to believe
you call the shots.

A newborn zoo elephant reaches
for his mother's milk,
unaware a rugged fence
defines the limits of their lives.

Yet animals are not vindictive,
often coming to our rescue
despite what we do
to them.

Just before a tsunami hit
Thailand in 2004,
eight elephants broke their chains
and carried eight tourists to safety.

We expect them to love us,
train them to do
what we will not do
for ourselves.

The captive jaguar has given up
trying to make it past
the invisible boundary
constraint imposes.

The rattler coils and raises it tail,
its tongue darting in and out
of a mouth designed
for terminal punishment.

Wildebeests and zebras run together
on the African savannah,
each knowing it has an instinct
the other needs.

The bear leading her cubs
from hibernation
cannot know she is about to step
into the cruel trap of agony.

A humpback's song haunts oceans
despite the sonar
sounding through
its depths.

A once-wild horse feels the bit
in his mouth and remembers
running with other horses
across a landscape of freedom.

That large black crow sitting on a
telephone wire with other crows
invents a story
we cannot imagine,

while an ant, one in a colony of thousands,
thinks and acts in unison,
its behavior programmed
by some larger law.

We humans alone design fences and walls
of our own making, sad punctuation
for the creative genius
we might enlist.

Becoming Ourselves

Where we go next depends upon a landscape
etched by wind.

Color sings, a golden sax paints purple
on orange cliffs.

Climbing or descending, brown spars with green
behind our eyes.

Clashing childhood stories send us
in different directions.

Becoming ourselves, we begin to move
toward one another.

Promises sing anthems
in our veins.

Temperature is a magnet in bodies
that yearn.

Now we are closer to the exit
than the launch

and the questions still weigh more
than the answers.

Where we go next depends upon a landscape
etched by wind.

Every Morning

Every morning, dependable as a baby's innocent scent,
light floods through horizontal blinds
bringing with it narrow stripes of other buildings
where other people are waking
to the shapes and songs of city life.

Mid-summer the light arrives, and I know it must be
five-thirty or thereabouts. As the great ball spins
steadily away from our flaming star
the darts of light come later and my eyes
search their horizons.

Imagining those bands uncurling from a tight spring,
their colors imprinting themselves upon my skin.
I am reduced by what I cannot see: rubble
where war undoes integrity, sounds and smells
invade the waking dream.

And I know the calm between my blinds is illusion
torn from rattled memory, dangerous
as melting icecaps or human avarice, a language
that might be satisfied with privilege
but isn't.

Directionality is the answer to every yearning question,
the place from which you look
and the one you inhabit
as others strain their eyes between their blinds
and look at you.

Are you the one whose jaw cracked beneath his fist
or did you lunge and connect,
trading your words for brute force as taught
by presidents and gurus: the DNA of violence
in your blood?

I ask myself if I will go out each morning
with conformity, that deadly sameness,
or if on some unexpected day I will gaze
in astonishment at change, welcoming me
at last to more than survival.

From Where I Stand

From where I stand it's a long road
through broken doors,
salt flats abrading the tongue.

A word uncurls, throws off its shroud
and wipes the salt from its lips,
breathing hard.

Another approaches, says its piece
despite that acrid barrage
aimed at its tenderest places.

Sticks and stones, the ditty goes,
claiming themselves weapons
while words wait impatient.

A foolish song, like so many
aimed at our innocence
and taking a lifetime to unlearn.

House of Battered Hope

*On occasion of the US withdrawal
from Afghanistan, August 2021.*

Aaina's name means mirror. If she
looks in one, she sees
imprisonment, and prison too
for her daughter sleeping innocent
in her crib. Giti means world or universe.
Hers has been reduced to her burqa's
window of damp mesh.

At Kabul University a professor
dismisses his Friday class.
I'll see you next week, he tells the men
and *I guess we won't see each other again*
are the sorrowful words
he speaks to the women.
They all know why.

The long war that didn't need to be
rewards us with a quarter million
dead and every human hope
betrayed.
Fundamentalism bided its time,
waited until the occupying force
had enough.

On the heels of an invading army's
retreat, those turbaned men
who believe they are God's chosen
take every village and city
until they arrive at the capital
leaving those who thought they could flee
dropping from the wings of departing planes.

It's no longer about whether this war
should have been fought
to begin with, what it cost
in lives and treasure,
or how we count the dead—
including only our own
or every casualty.

No, these are not the right questions
and we cannot know
the right questions
living as we do in another century,
remembering the fall of Saigon
and pondering
its lingering trail.

I am tired of informed analysis against
a backdrop of open wounds
and broken promises.
We talk and talk while they are
forced to invisibility,
made to walk a gauntlet of fear,
become a bullseye of regret.

The name Amena means safe
but she is not safe.
Mothers and aunts, sisters
and girl children: all
have become once more
a tired book in which
death's recipe is written.

Every Afghan has regressed to a time
before Illumination, when free will
belongs to no one,
the men who take control
as birthright or the women and girls
left carrying memory
to a house of battered hope.

Not an Occasional Poem

For Barbara.

That remembered place
we call *before*
woven of emptiness and longing
stares back in disbelief.

Before you showed up
in your purple overalls
and yellow sneakers
riding a motorcycle

named Virginia after
your mother
who suffered from MS,
and carrying a cane to juggle

your own
insubordinate neurology.
Twenty years in
you finally shed the shaming curls.

I hold your brilliant mind
in my grateful hands,
cherish the words you write
in unreadable script.

Now we are approaching thirty-six.
Before is the memory
of yes
and then again yes.

After keeps on blooming along
its pathway of change
and we discover we are the change
we have been waiting for.

How Are You?

How are you? he asks but isn't prepared
for you to tell him
your little brother's last words were
I can't breathe, gasped whisper
beneath a rogue cop's knee.

His cheerful tone doesn't expect
you to say your mother died
of COVID because the hospital
ran out of ventilators
and she was triaged as too old.

Not so good today is never a welcome
response. Better to reply *Fine,
thank you, and you?*
Then you too may cultivate
the lie.

Smoke screens passing as conversation
in an era when uttering words
that mean what they say
would be like cutting your wrists
and watching the blood flow.

The Smile Trembling on My Lips

When flesh abandons the mirror
that once returned a reflection
of youthful deception,
then graceful change moved
from maturity's elegance
to the harbor of aged wisdom,
I stop to absorb the story.

I force myself to contemplate
the scaly patch of skin
on one bony shoulder,
the bags of wrinkles hanging
from each arm, multiple chins
and gardens of stiff hair
sprouting everywhere.

On my head what was once
a lush crown is thin
and colorless, combed this way
and that in hopeful subterfuge.
The clear blue of younger eyes
has faded to milky gray
beneath a bothered brow.

I have a choice: either paint,
tweeze, chisel and mold,
supporting an industry that reaps
billions with curdled promises,
or learn to love the map
of a journey that sings
in the manner of an old violin.

I have opted for the latter
while freely admitting
to moments when fantasy
breaks through this façade
of resistance,
riding roughshod over the smile
defiant on my lips.

Prepared to Invade
the Next Receptive Host

Need relaxes, settles against the cold metal lumbar
of one of those benches conveniently placed
along this garden path. Need is waiting there,
prepared to invade the next receptive host.

Hunger and cold have easier jobs. There is always
someone who's missed a meal or must beg
for enough to buy the blue plate special at the diner
that refuses them entrance, makes them wait at the door.

If all the shelter beds are taken and a body already
inhabits the spot beside the subway grate,
cold has every advantage and may kill
before the first ray of sun turns threat around.

But need is smug, all-knowing. Experience tells her
she can reach beyond temperature, is not reduced
to the salivating tongue in a dry mouth
or sores claiming exhausted skin.

Need remembers a time of wonder, a place alive
with dreams. At home on her bench
she whispers sweet nothings in the ears
of all those threatened by forgetting.

She tells anyone who listens there's no such thing
as simple want, no desperation so numb
it doesn't dream in brilliant color or imagine a world
where everyone dresses for the season, walks upright.

Hope or Yope

I thought I was striking the H
but the Y started
showing up instead.
I'm talking about the keyboard
on my computer
like the typewriter years before:
extension of fingertips and brain.

This wasn't supposed to happen
and instead of a momentary
blip it repeats itself,
becomes routine
until I expect my forefinger
will come down
on the wrong key.

I am trying to solve this puzzle
of disobedience or deceit,
understand why
my right hand goes rogue
every time.
Do I blame arthritis,
age or some other disconnect?

I wonder because these days
I write *yope*
when I mean *hope*
and don't know whether
I've invented a new word
or simply feel more alienated
from the one I meant to write.

All Those Years Ago

Have you ever wondered
what a simple change,
say for example your teacher
all those years ago
greeting the class
good morning girls and boys
instead of *boys and girls*,
might have done
for your
self-esteem?

Have you ever imagined
blue—electric or sky,
seafoam or periwinkle
or any of the radiant shades
morphing to purple
as it flees navy—
rather than that insipid pink
absorbing your breath
and giving nothing back?

Is it too late to undo
every assumption,
each alluring prescription
stamped and sealed
in its glittering wrapper,
seduction its weapon
as it wrings you dry
one infinitesimal turn
of the screw at a time?

Are you able to step away,
look back or down,
as the case may be,
and take a quiet breath?
Changed expectation
offers a changed reality
as surely as opening a window
invites fresh air
into a musty room.

Notice the bridge. It will
encourage you
to walk across.
Accept that the thunderhead
may bring a wall of mud
or tumbling branches
along with refreshing rain.
It is part of the risk
and its promise is everything.

The Playground See-Saw

On the playground see-saw we learned
a child of equal weight
could keep us balanced in crisp fall air.
Lighter, and we wouldn't rise.
Heavier, and we might remain up there forever.

Little did we know that playful diversion
was teaching us something
we'd need to know in later life: how
influencing another's energy
requires being able to access our own.

What began as play returns as a lesson
from an old friend
who has only to punch you good-naturedly
or utter a few familiar words
and you get the message.

On the vast and complex map of my years
I search for cause and effect
in twisting canyons and abandoned mines.
They hide in plain sight or come
to lick my face like an over-friendly dog.

Dressing the Part

Scarsdale clad my sister and me
in paisley prints,
matching bodices, empire waists
and Peter Pan collars: dresses
that screamed the culture that constrained us,
no questions asked.

We moved west, and I got an allowance,
lessons about the money's value
and the virtue of saving. Choice, but within
the limits of our class
and how a proper young lady
was supposed to look.

I wanted the mother-of-pearl buttons
on the tight-fitting western shirt
proclaiming I belonged to this exotic place
where mountains rose from the desert
leaving sandstorms
in their wake.

I longed for a tiny Barbie waist,
cashmere sweater set
and stiff crinoline, shiny coins
in the slots of my penny loafers
or saddle shoes laced upside down
signaling young love's commitment.

Fleeing the pain of adolescence,
I embraced those
brightly threaded blouses
indigenous women call *huipiles*,
ignorant theirs told life stories
while mine were mute.

I learned each season's demands
for the latest fashion
didn't dress us better
but clothed an industry in profit,
assigning charity to the poor
and vintage to the privileged renegade.

An imposter in academia bought
years of professorial suits.
Attired like the men who still earned
twice as much as we did.
Fraternity of tweed
to level a lifetime of inequality.

Now it's Levi's and a black shirt all day
every day, short-sleeved
in summer, long in winter,
no makeup
but my signature turquoise
hanging from each ear.

This uniform of resistance refuses
to surrender
what a skewed system demands.
I won't dress the part
or cooperate in any further way.
I will not play their game.

Our Future Tense

Industrious never wanted
to be a noun.
It gazes in awe
at other words, proud
to be verbs
or sassy little articles.

Lazy doesn't mind being used
to stigmatize nouns,
confident as it is
of being a verb at heart.
Tone of voice is everything,
it explains to anyone listening.

Brilliant claims it may precede
or follow the word it adorns,
adding that extra glow
or spicing up a mundane idea
when confidence
is lacking.

Our vocabulary isn't to blame
for bad jokes,
self-serving anecdotes
and fanciful speeches.
But our words do precede us
into future tense.

Our Humanness

Law brings out its sharp knives
carving and cutting
how we view one another
when one is darker or lighter,
another braves a dangerous border,
others love who they love,
risk be damned.

Then there's the human response,
a neighbor risking life itself
to hide the boy
whose missing foreskin
betrays original sin
or the girl who went silent
when they took her parents.

No law negates our loving
one another
nurturing the tree
where sweet fruits grow
enough to satiate
all our dreams, our will, our risk,
our humanness.

It Matters

One for Zoilamérica Ortega.

"...the fruit of thy womb..."
—*Hail Mary (Catholic prayer)*

We are alone or together
in this great wild sea
of the cosmos we observe
with our eyes, hear with our ears.

Shakespeare's Lady Macbeth has no
children but tells the monarch
she will kill the fruit of her womb
if he asks.

In Nicaragua a mother gives birth
to nine,
proving year after year
fulfillment of her role.

When a daughter reveals
her stepfather's rape
the mother doesn't hesitate
to sacrifice the girl.

A wife siding with her husband
is a common story
except for this wife it is power
rather than security.

Alone in the great wild sea
of the cosmos
or human to human,
it matters.

Two for the Price of One

Another for Zoilamérica Ortega.

Two for the price of one, the mother
lent the daughter to her husband,
turned away when the daughter rebelled.
What did the mother get?
A share in his power.
The daughter's rape deemed private,
collateral damage at best.

Power's sickness can destroy
the most beautiful dream
and turn it to dust,
betray days
without enough to eat,
each drop of willing blood,
every life given generously.

Father and mother took control
of a nation,
imprisoned or exiled anyone opposed
to their crimes.
Daughter was the dress rehearsal,
an exercise to gauge support.
She lives in another country now.

"Everything Will Be All Right"

Problems abound, deep swamps
grabbing at your feet,
pulling you to a place
where escape is impossible
and you must give something up
in exchange for avoiding
sure death.

Miracle remedies seduce
from the sidelines
claiming aphoristic fixes
in short sentences.
The Universe provides a positive
for every negative may make you feel
better for a while.

Put down that book promising
comfort for $39.95.
The only truthful part of the deal
is the profit that accrues
to Amazon.com with perhaps
a bit to publisher, distributor,
maybe writer.

Those Hallmark sayings may bring
momentary relief—a breather
sustained in hope—
but when you close the book
Ida's waters still drown your home,
the Caldor fire still threatens,
no hospital bed to be had.

All you need do is look to history,
millennia of humans
unleashing their power
against the weak
or simply those who are different:
repetition of evil despite a chorus
of *we will never forget*.

It's up to us. Come on now. We need
your strong shoulders
at the wheel,
capable hands and, yes, also
your ideas born of experience,
willing to move with other ideas
steering us through these times.

Life Is a Two-Way Street

Diné weavers often leave
a weft of wool
running to the rug's edge:
a pathway out.

Those who follow
that strand
know freedom
when it touches them.

But finding your way in
requires identical risk
as being able to escape.
Life is a two-way street.

What I Think and Feel

There are times the poem holds back
from the page, hesitates
to declare itself indelible
despite my relentless insistence.

It knows once it appears—black words
inscribed on white paper—
it will enter the world's memory,
no going back.

I may reach for it, word by word
or letter by letter,
pushing and shoving
to hurry it along.

I embrace its tired shoulders, tell it lies
to get it moving,
so that what I think and feel
may live in the world.

The poem reminds me then
it owes me nothing.
I am beholden to it
in this season of acid rain.

I still believe we are partners,
the poem and me.
If we could just work together
through our moment in the sun.

My Theory of Nothing

They are excited by a Theory of Everything,
gravity to the tiniest sub-particle
of cosmic dust,
something to explain where we come from,
where we are going
and what we have learned
along the way.

Like a giant jigsaw, the placid lake
assembles easily
but its shore is still torn by empty spaces
and the surrounding mountains
are missing gaping holes
yet to be filled. We cannot see
the connections.

I am searching for a Theory of Nothing,
not explanation
so much as remedy
for all that is wrong
with this system and its million
grasping claws tearing our limbs
from hunger.

My pot of gold at the end of a neon rainbow
beckons with a smile,
snuggles up to the passion
hiding in a nearby poem
or the rich earth
young children turn over
with toy shovels.

Those guys in their garments of privilege
share a grand goal, ambition
trampling community gardens
in an age when patriarchy
keeps the big prizes
for the fast food
musketeers.

But Everything shivers this bleak
winter night,
asks how we imagine
the infinite and infinitesimal
can inhabit the same sentence.
For once they find themselves
out in the cold.

A Theory of Nothing folds me
into its arms,
murmurs secrets that fill the silences
they endeavor to protect.
Remedy, please, I repeat,
as I move from sleep
to grasp the nearest hand.

The Sum of One and One

The earth was barren,
battered by centuries
of greed
and salt of abandon.

The poet insisted on planting a word,
nurturing its hesitant roots
and dreaming the rain
that would bring it life.

That single word grew lonely
at times, dependent
on the poet's
nurturing memories.

Once the word stood strong
on its windswept home
the poet planted
another.

She taught them collaboration
and that the sum of
one and one is always
more than two.

Time passed and returned
with unexpected gifts.
A field of words reaches for
meaning among the weeds.

The words are a poem now,
its rhythms piercing
a million ears crowding close
that they may hear.

Understanding Metaphor

Without a sense of humor about
where Jesus was baptized
when warring countries claim the spot,

without understanding metaphor
when it comes to raising the dead
or that production line of bread and fish,

without the patience to follow a darkling beetle
on its labored journey through sand
or watch the dance as light and shadow

switch places in a picture-perfect landscape
as night descends and dreams
fill the canyons behind your eyes,

you may have become a handmaiden
without noticing privilege
is gone for good.

On Life's Rickety Stages

I declare myself still here, beating heart
and insatiable curiosity
not shaped by faith or rules
but forged at the margins of their blasphemy.

Beneath a trapdoor in the floorboards
of a German farmhouse
a Jewish child's whisper
scratches my throat as I speak.

My sentences rise an octave at the end,
their Spanish lilt preceding me
on life's rickety stages
singing the impossible.

These days desert heat warms me
cholla blooming in my arms
the walls of its slot canyons
sustaining my slowing steps.

Some memories bring nightmares
shattering sleep
to the staccato of rusty machine-gun fire,
leaving a taste of metal in my mouth.

Children who exploded between my thighs
gave birth to children of their own
who bring theirs into a world
that still needs fixing.

As I prepare for the inevitable exit
I nurture a hope that saner winds
may clear all children's dreams
of such debris.

One Direction or Another

An outstretched hand
is as distant
from the clenched fist
as your sunny neighborhood
from China.

The child who digs straight down
is sure she will rise
from her tunnel of anticipation
into a place where words
look at her and laugh.

She is pushed in one direction
or another
compelled by crimes
committed before her birth.
They whisper in her ears

even when she sleeps,
she is surrounded
by their thunderous rage
but she can make it stop.
She just doesn't know it yet.

When I Die

When I die if you speak of me
at all please say I am dead.
Do not use phrases like
transitioned or *passed on*
or describe me as
moving toward the light.

I never lived in darkness
although darkness
often came knocking at my door
trying to lure me
onto its path
of lazy impersonation.

I always resisted, stumbled and
fell but picked myself up,
brushed deceptive lies
from denim pants
and steadied my breath
for the journey ahead.

I want to know death
as I knew life:
full throttle and conscious
of its idiosyncrasies,
as uniquely mine as
my chosen culture prescribes.

We may comfort ourselves
with fantasies
that calm our spirits,
warm our fearful minds.
Truth is my faithful lover,
balm for every doubt.

Still, you may be surprised
to know my certainty
also possesses its quota
of magic,
landscape of wonder
in cosmic energy.

Over and Out

Over and out is a temporary farewell,
dependable as the perennial bloom
that comes back year after year.

Despite its name, the century plant
or *Agave americana* produces
a flower at twenty, then dies.

We of the human species think about
our final goodbye, imagine an exit
echoing with wisdom

or at least some comfort for those
we leave behind. If we get there
without memory

the best-laid plans may have been
in vain. Good intentions and all,
we must wait and see.

Beyond

We try to imagine the landscape
without us, glib reward
decked out in one of those flavors
advertised by systems
designed to cancel
the boredom of nothing.

Nothing at all is my bet
when it comes
to the impossible.
I opt for what I cannot know:
my earthbound mind okay
with not being able to go beyond.

How to see the unseeable,
hear notes higher
or lower than the ear absorbs,
touch what flees from
hopeful fingers
or hides from intuition?

We may withdraw from sensation,
reach for a limitless emptiness,
nothing to hold us together,
no familiar feel
on the surface of weathered skin,
nothing out there but time

with no clock to sing its hours,
no minutes advancing
in eyes that believe
they have seen it all,
movement in
the only conceivable direction.

We remain immobile in the center,
winds of everything or nothing
blowing about us, dancing
or marching to their own tune.
A vast unknown
hiding while daring us to look.

From here to there is a territory
we explore, proud we're
adventurous enough
to defy the comfort of gravity.
From there to here is the question:
humble in all its mystery.

Learning to Think
about Hunger and Want

There is always something more
if you scrape the barrel
or clean your plate—*children
are starving in Europe*
I was told when, a child myself,
I wondered how my leftovers
would be sent to them.

A generation later we told
our own: *children
are starving in Africa*
and they too wondered
about the logistics
but learned to think
about hunger and want.

Compassion continues to duel
with a sense of self
as alone and enraged
in a world primed to win
at any cost. There will always
be hunger while we debate
what we can give

or worry about how to get it
to its destination.
There will always be
self-centered rage
while we pretend
any war has winners
and losers.

Never the Compliment It Pretends

For all those who are forced from their homes
by terror or want and never completely arrive
in the promised land.

Where you from? the fine edge of a razorblade
beneath your nails or an innocent question
hiding behind the clown's sad mask—greasepaint
smudged as it leers its happy face.

The immigrant pronounces her country's name
in almost perfect English. She's practiced
before a mirror in which she struggles
to find herself.

The questioner may turn away or say *that's nice*
or tell her she doesn't look like people
from there, which is never the compliment
it pretends.

Hollywood's promise turns faded celluloid
at a neighborhood cineplex
where the smell of stale popcorn
clings to her thrift shop garb.

And the person who endured years of paperwork
or crossed beneath the cover of night
is no longer from there and will never
completely be here.

She remembers the texture of rain, waves beating
against a broken sea wall, feel of air
on her face or that homegrown hardship
familiar to her hands.

Those memories grow distant as the years unfold
and her daughter's distant eyes
greet her when she tells the stories
she keeps beneath her pillow.

Respect for the Word

Respect for the word promises
a place where it may live
without pain of censure
or shame of an existence,
bereft of meaning.

Saying what we mean and
exactly what we mean
is a job well done,
cadence as steady as heartbeat
fighting hurricane surf.

A father who slaps his son
across the face, a mother
threatening to wash her daughter's
mouth out with soap, stifle future's
grace and power.

Words grow and mature, marry
others from far-off places
create vibrations
that describe
our passions and our grief.

Respect for the word is respect
for memory
yet to be written on the feedback loop
of a history we write with our blood
each day.

Memory Tattoos Numbers on My Skin

That soft place where I felt secure
shows signs of distress
along its edges: fissures and faults.
Mirror's wait-time fills with demons.
Memory tattoos numbers on my skin.
Cries for help echo in my ears.
A loved one's eyes take my breath away.

I thought I was safe, rent and utilities
paid on that small strip of land
where storms can't kill or maim.
Now I enter a room
and conversation stops.
I hang from my thumbs
in a silence that measures oblivion.

It isn't the betrayal itself that hurts
but its suddenness,
a departure I didn't expect,
neither goodbyes nor a gentle island
on which to lay my head.
When opportunity lures, the smug dig in
for the duration.

Monotony of Repetition
and Passion of Repair

There are things we do not share
with the world,
intimate moments, ours alone.
The temperature of bodies
touching,
the way they still nest

one beside the other, years spooning
despite loosening flesh
extra poundage
calendars brought to task
by exhaustion of hope.

There are things we don't say
except in the lover's ear,
stories whispered
with all the monotony of repetition
and passion of repair.

Those who offer their intimacies
to the world
believe they are generous. Perhaps.
We only know as far as our arms reach,
our words piercing a pushback of denial.

Saving Our Place in the Crowd

When *live in the moment* and *don't judge others*
deny our better selves
and barge into my life without knocking,
it's hard to breathe.

Some say they are glad to be old, won't be around
for the holocaust threatening complacency,
sharpening its teeth
on our ragged resistance.

But what about the young ones, I ask,
and those not yet born
whose stories depend on what we do today
that they may thrive?

I stumble over a child's broken bicycle.
The stench of rotting garbage
trips me as I fall, echoes from the future
we dare to imagine now.

That daring imagination might be enough
if arrows of frozen pain
didn't zero in,
memory sneaking up on us.

We ignore the plight of others,
then forty-foot waves
batter the beaches where we believed
we were safe from collapsing bridges.

Words sound good until action is required.
A moment we didn't expect.
Pushed to a higher common denominator,
we lower our voices

to a whisper, don that old suit of clothes
with its patches of sky
and wind filling sleeves ripe with confession,
saving our place in the crowd.

The Heart Muscle

For my daughter Ximena.

The heart muscle drags other muscles
in its fervent wake,
urging a journey of obedience
through the acrobatics of age.

The mind muscle glimpses silhouettes
and shadows, places
where synapses try to connect,
surprising old cloth with brilliant color.

A daughter asks if she was anxious
as an infant. She is traveling
the back roads she hopes will explain
today's dilemmas.

A friend won't reveal the year
she was born, cultivates
flowing tresses and imagery that renders her
younger, forever younger.

I fight a thin forest of Ho Chi Minh
hairs sprouting from my chin,
accept some ninth-decade changes,
suffer with others.

Age is the wise coyote laughing behind
that bend in the canyon
you will reach only if you let yourself
tumble in freefall down the mountainside.

Tragic Flaw

I come from a place that tried to quench its thirst
with empty promises, billboards
thrusting lies between cracked lips and a breastbone
hinged to hope.

Land where I once walked to school, sand shards
biting my strong young calves
as I gave myself to life, all of it answers
and yes.

Now every answer spawns a question, babies
with too many fingers or toes
and brains too small to grapple with such problems
remind of us of moments missed.

The grossly obese in their plastic palaces suck residue
of moisture from my habitat, not even water now
but pale shards of what once satiated our pheromones
in free-fall.

I come from a place where two and two was always
four, reason didn't try to hide
behind self-beating breasts bludgeoning us
with their repeated lies.

We thought for ourselves back then, aiming volleys
of simple words that didn't pretend to be
what they were not. Stoking counterfeit desire
we waited.

And that was our tragic flaw, the dangerous wishbone
in my throat. Waiting is fallback unable
to take a breath, leading us to a place where
we cannot trust ourselves.

Now my land's patchwork puzzle of poison cracks
swallows us whole and only poetry sings
on fertile ground, the chance to go back, do it over,
survive.

Desert

Wind writes its autobiography in sand,
mummified mesquite sap
inking millennial rock, turning
dry riverbeds to intimate history.

Wild English gardens may tilt their heads
and lift their aristocratic chins
enveloped in the watery fog
of nurturing rains.

The French cut their hedges
in perfect shapes,
patterning nature to reflect
their sense of reason.

Here the fuchsia blossoms on a cholla
cling resolutely to its withered arm,
proud agaves flower once
every decade.

On deserts the Welwitschia with its two
lonely leaves or bristlecone pine
are the exclamation points
moving the story past sage and cedar.

Giant trunks of ancient trees turn
to agate, their petrified colors
waiting to be washed by the next
great flood or future sea.

Canyon walls lick voluptuous lips of fire
where color explodes
to the rhythms of a disappearing sun
that leaves no heat behind.

Patience is required to read this memoir
of life and death, eons of beauty
at a single hungry glance
on a canvas too vast to digest.

The Acequias

The acequias are dry, dust blowing
where water once ran,
dead alfalfa, corn stalks
bearing sad ears, blighted kernels.

The news came first in sweeping
predictions: photos of
cracked earth and sinking water tables,
millions of plastic bottles deformed.

Then neighbors spoke of dying farms,
their losses touching you
where regret pinches your flesh
with its bony fingers.

This morning you turn the handle
above your sink and nothing
issues from the spigot
but the hiss of parched regret.

Meanwhile, a multi-billion-dollar
space program announces
the discovery of water on Mars
in small but promising quantities.

Water's Desire

Scientists now believe
they've discovered
water has memory,

each drop containing
its unique pattern
resulting

from where it has been
what moves it forward
and what it carries.

Water speaks, telling
its own story
of pain or desire.

My tears are encyclopedic,
bursting with absence,
loss and the joy

that overflows reason.
They make their way
down the ravines of my face.

Their memories chew the meat
on my bones as they dry
and wait to feed another season.

Earth's Dawn and Mine

Early morning on any day
I rub night's loam
from my eyes
and Earth's dawn
pulls me into its embrace.

Forgotten seas, virgin forests
where dew coats
the leaves of giant ferns
and sun's light
is beyond human reach.

This is the beginning of time,
a conceit that cracks
beneath the insistence of memory,
hopeful diorama
embedded in our eyes.

Recreating ourselves in each
brave act,
we still leave
infinite hearts behind
beating in infinity of breasts.

Inhabiting the wreckage,
we struggle to avoid
the confusion
of bungling,
our cacophony's desire.

I Want to Glimpse
the Woman Giving Birth

Technology burrows under
a millennium's overgrowth,
peers beneath earth and rain
to reveal alluring outlines
of plazas, houses, theaters,
fields and walls:
definition of community.

Lidar combines radar and light
to map a world long gone
to speculation, lost imprint
of those who worked and loved,
played and died and gave birth.
Progress rewards
our curiosity.

I trace the emerging patterns
of people who walked
so long ago, bring
their images to my lips,
cast my net for bits and pieces
clinging to the soles
of silent feet.

But I wait for a discovery
that will give me
memory as it traces fault lines
and homes, a map obliterated
by the one upon which we live
as the earth, wounded
by our ignorance, turns upon itself.

I want to glimpse the woman
giving birth, a lover's smile
or kiss, even the slap
a man hurled across his woman's face,
the lilt of a winter melody.
I want more than outlines and walls.
I want life.

Words as Breadcrumbs

One word leads to another,
trail of breadcrumbs
in feedback loop
to their origins.

Some are always running
to catch up
while others amble along
at their own pace.

Memory may skip a syllable,
keeping M or Z
from overshadowing L
or doubling up at times.

My words inhabit their power
when they say
what they mean,
fallout be damned.

After decades imitating those voices
of authority
each word spoken in resistance
proudly claims its place.

It's not automatic, though,
still depends on me
to show them
where to stand,

how to enter the minds
of those who
need their energy:
gentle nudge or wild epiphany.

Codependence of Light and Shadow

Light circles shadow's terrain
leading shadow to believe
it can dull its twin's perfect pitch
by simple confrontation.

Moving through water, light keeps
its distance,
illuminating a path that may
separate you from yourself.

On currents of spring air,
it targets a bullseye
in perpetual motion,
changing position on whim.

In autumn it takes to its bed,
pale and worn,
and we horde what we can
for the months to come.

Those who are blind project
untethered images
in mirrors of imagination,
live in that world where shadow reigns.

On ancient stone, light's dagger
descends in tandem
with celestial bodies,
telling us where we are.

Insecure because they know
they reflect our brilliance,
light and shadow are
the essence of codependence.

Give Yourself Up to Friendly Currents

If you oversalt the soup there's always sugar,
a pinch will marry sweet to savory
achieving the perfect answer to any excess.

If you swim too far from shore, don't fight
the waves but give yourself up
to friendly currents, bright energy of trust.

If your last lie floundered like fish on
a slippery deck, don't tell another
until old scores are settled and forgotten.

Love's promises are simple, but remember
history's unexpected turns,
experience's habit of getting in the way.

There are times it's better to stand back,
survey the elevation contour lines
on your survey map and let muscle memory

take you where it will. Ecstasy may be
another name for that target
with arrows piercing its heart.

The Other

From in here, her hand on my naked back
whispers the way she knows me,
temperature to temperature,
excitement and lasting comfort
weaving our narrative.

From out there, I cannot know
what she feels: how much
of my heat or calm comes through,
the texture of skin dried and creased by age,
sackcloth replacing silk.

It's the same when I touch her, the territory
between us still unknown, mysterious.
After all these years, we experience the other
only from where we are
and how we inhabit that place.

Just People

The generational spiral rises grumpy at times,
graceful at others and, despite all platitudes,
it's the curdled moments
reveal those hidden directions
on your map.

Father was Everyman and Mother his helpmeet,
sweetheart or whore as their fairytale required,
patterns imprinted on your breath
like monsoon rains.
Or maybe it was the other way around.

Your home wasn't like the others, after all,
pampered secrets at the ready.
Their smug narrative held your hands
to the fire,
sealed with a smile.

When you had your own children, you vowed
correctives worthy of the experts,
I'll never do this or say that, you said, *always
be there when they need me.*
Promises like drunken darts.

When the grandchildren arrived, you observed
the rekindled parent/child dance,
awed by continuity, shocked
when a daughter hid in silence or lies.
Defense of the innocent.

From time to time you think of your parents,
the temperature of Dad's aging hand
in yours, finishing Mom's sentence
or her finishing yours.
Memories turned inside out.

The family joke that had you wild with glee
when you were nine
floats aimlessly on an empty landscape
if you repeat it today.
Time stumbles over its own feet.

You think of your parents, gone decades
now, still speak of them as you
always have, words aiming to reproduce
the feel of summer.
Familiarity switches its disguise.

Then one day—you are closer to gone yourself—
a mirror falls and breaks:
they were Mother and Father
but they were also people,
just people living their legacies of pain.

Moving Page after Ragged Page

*"When you die, there's either nothing,
in which case I'm finished,
or there's something."*

—*Jane Goodall**

Gifts have been bountiful
to my years—
a first family that harvested love
from inherited weeds, men
and then finally a woman
who loves me enough
for the duration.

Children arriving one by one
to share what I give
and return the gift one-thousandfold,
their children
and their children's children:
unbroken line
stretching from my hands.

A taste of war painful enough
to show me the virtues
of peace.
Enough in trade
that I've never had to choose
between warm clothes
and a hot meal.

And then this limitless supply
of blank paper
where I write what I think and feel,
erase and deliver it again.
I am the most fortunate of beings
moving page after ragged page
through this calendar of my life.

*In an interview with Tara Parker-Pope, *New York Times*,
October 23, 2021.

In Remembrance

Make it small. Invisible. Store it in a tiny device
where a thousand books reside
and one click of the cursor greets you
with full-color cover, variable type size,
background either black on white,
white on black or a calming
shade of gray.

Make the word itself brief as you can,
a single exclamatory example
like *cool* is all you need in response
to any situation. Even *huh* can stand as
a question now, or *hmm* make do,
no actual thought required
for meaning's sake.

Make it quick. No need to waste time or
tell the story from start to finish,
retrieve memory from its hiding place,
coax it to dance in your jaded eyes
or swim to the far shore of an ocean
of mimicry, only to emerge brushing sand
from your naked body.

Be modern, keep up with your children
who know nothing else,
have never seen a book
but in a museum, never held
its precious weight in hand
or smelled the endurance of ink
across its pages.

Make it efficient, practical. No need
for leather bindings,
scent of centuries, titles embossed in gold,
tissue-thin end papers and nameplates
no one cares about today.
And when there are no more books
who will want bookstores?

No one will have time to browse through
their stacks so libraries too
will be delights of the past, everything
can be done from home,
that is if you have a home
and don't dream of taking refuge
in places where wonder lives.

Take My Breath and Turn It Inside Out

For some who mistakenly think they are poets.

It's poetry time and I am
on the edge of my seat,
waiting for its magic
to grab me,
spin me, blast me,
pick me up like Dorothy
and set me down in Kansas.

Like many I was taught
if you can't say
something nice, don't
say anything at all
by elders whose putdowns
came in every shape
and size.

I know the risks of honesty
when saying
what one really thinks
comes back to bite
teeth that bare themselves
and lips that lick
a saccharine regret.

I want to love your poems
but find your references
self-serving,
metaphors repetitious,
rhythms derivative
and the colors of your words
opaque.

The poem is not rehearsal
or therapy, it doesn't
lie down and obey
but rises irreverent in your throat.
You must dig deep
and climb high,
or I won't be there at the end.

Don't tell me about it, describe
what happened
or why.
Worse: don't explain the poem
before you read it.
Make me live the experience
myself.

I don't know where your images
come from,
only that they fade
on a map that yearns to follow
where you've gone,
where you struggle now
and what it costs.

I want to clap but my hands
weigh too much,
won't come together
in applause.
They will answer to nothing
but an energy
that shakes them loose.

I need language that is clear
but beautiful,
words that move
in unexpected ways,
moments that take
my breath and turn it
inside out.

Your books sell out, your work
is in every anthology
and you've won all the grants.
Nothing left
to look forward to then
but the Nobel
and blowing my mind.

Words in the Fun House Mirror

The word *memory* entered my vocabulary
disguised as a bridge. When bare feet
ran across it, the broken slats beneath their weight
separated slightly and I could see a river,
its ferocious rapids raging below.

When the word *memory* came into my life
disguise had lost its allure.
I still had to cross that bridge.
I didn't look down but only straight ahead
until I was safely on the other side.

What we read in books or hear on the lips
of others never prepares us for those
real-life experiences that threaten to change
our shape and temperature, sometimes
even giving us a brand-new name.

The word *forgive* holds no interest for me.
I prefer the word *judge*, of ill repute
and shunned by many but useful
when rocket blasts scar the horizon
and crops are ripe for harvest.

No One Washes Their Hands

Somewhere beneath my left temple
the Middle Ages tries
to spread its unruly borders.
There is so much disease
and no one
washes their hands.

Between my ribs horses pull carriages
over roads of petrified stone.
Motors are futile fantasies
in wild imaginations
and equine lungs expand and contract
in rhythm with the times.

In one swollen knee, prehistoric seas
lap shores on which animals
long extinct devour others
in a chain that may or may not
spell justice or confirm
our knowledge of prehistory.

Rivers run the length of my fingers
to fertile deltas, slavery's
mournful music haunting a future
called Mississippi
where trade and hunger and pain
collide at the base of my thumb.

We have the fossils and footprints,
carbon and other methods
for accurate dating, disciplines
that may not speak to each other
but pour data into dioramas
reflecting wistful lies.

My body holds it all. If only I could
decipher this arthritic stiffness
or sudden headache,
the persistent itch at that spot
I cannot reach, the bruises
blossoming on my skin.

No Longer the Color of Promise

We are in the museum's twenty-first-century wing
featuring an exhibit of period cars,
face masks and fashion for all genders:
an emphasis on loose-fitting garments
accelerating in seconds from flood to fire.

The label by that photograph of land art
describes its evolution through
what we once called seasons,
parch of summer and winter snow
responding to calendar months.

Newsreels of wars no side won
and what we used to call
collateral damage, those not supposed
to die. Now we know everyone dies
in a war except

the illustrious leaders safe behind
their titanium desks. Here is
a statue removed from its pedestal
and here the pedestal covered with what
were considered obscenities back then.

Viewers who enter these doors look in wonder
at a world their elders remember
when they think no one is listening, curiosity
building where memory is no longer
the color of promise.

The show is called *Believe It If You Can*.
One who stops to gaze
at a 5-D image looks at their friend
as if to say: *What were they thinking?*
The friend responds: *They weren't.*

Memory, Comforting or Brutal

"I was born before cell phones and computers,
before the proliferation of devices installed
with memory, which prompt the user to forget."

—*Joy Harjo**

A storm raging in every
internal organ
pummels muscle and sinew
on its ferocious
pilgrimage.

My body is a resonance chamber
on automatic,
as personal as this instant
of human production line
through time.

Hurricane broad as the horizon,
its deafening force
propelling that moment
pulling me
beyond myself.

Division of cells, zygote's blend
of DNA developing buds
that will become arms, legs, head:
embryo to newborn in perfect
synchrony.

Powerful enough to braid fear
with delight, a process
inhabiting my body
and keeping us both
on course.

Successive waves of pain
and euphoria
vibrate my knowing
until the warm wetness of calm
brings silence

pierced by the child's sudden cry,
freed from my flesh
and greeting a world
that imposes chance
on instinct.

Agony is gone from my memory
now, replaced
with dumb wonder
of anticipation, that condition
we call mothering.

Poet Warrior, page 12.

An erasure necessary
to the perpetuation
of the species, insuring
we will make the journey
again.

Memory, comforting or brutal
is only as willing
as its future place
on a scale that goes from zero
to infinity.

Breakthrough

Suddenly you get it, and it gets you.
You understand
and the breakthrough whets your parched lips
like water seeping through cracks
at the back of a cave
you know was home
ten thousand years ago.

This understanding is monumental,
cradles and rocks you
then goes still,
allowing its rivulets of knowledge
to enter your veins,
possess your body,
take you where you need to go.

Now you turn back to imagine
its opposite,
impossible challenge,
alter-ego
to that welcome sustenance
that tests the puzzle
with every piece in place.

You are reversing the answers
you received as a child
when they responded
to your questions
by telling you the devil
was speaking through you,
imprisoning you in fear.

They are gone now, floating
in that distance
where menacing winds lurk.
Now it's all you and only you
adding and subtracting,
free to cup your hands
against the moist rock of that wall.

Give that millennial water time
to cool your skin,
a chance to satiate your thirst
and deliver what you know
in a world
they no longer threaten
or control.

Humphrey Bogart's Trench Coat, Isadora Duncan's Scarf

Unless the unforeseen happens
I'll soon be eighty-six,
eighty-six springs, as some cultures tell it,
and I wonder if it's ever
eighty-six winters although the metaphor
might cause you to shiver
with sudden cold.

It's all good, as they say, but I admit
to surreptitious visits
to the *New York Times* obituaries
where I often find a friend
or acquaintance: shock piercing
the end of a sentence
lying in wait.

More than my own mortality,
with each loss I forfeit
a bit of myself: temperature of skin
on skin, kernel of memory
or elasticity of muscle, the sound
of a beloved's voice, eyes that hold mine
in tight embrace.

This is the first time I've written my age
in a poem. There was one
several years back in which three sentinels
harmonized a mantra
but they were lies, stand-ins
for moments marking the rhythm
of my years.

I can remember when I thought
an elder ancient at sixty:
tottering, dependent, dim about
the edges, halting in manner
and way beyond beautiful
or fit. Sixty was unknowable then,
the final act.

Today I wear these eight-and-
a-half decades like
Humphrey Bogart's trench coat
or Isadora Duncan's scarf
before it got caught
in the wheel of her motorcar.
My heart keeps perfect time.

If I gaze in the mirror with one eye
closed and squint through
the other, the reflection staring back
crowds my vision
with the innocent gauze
of impressionism's
ambitious palette.

I prefer to keep my eyes open,
coaxing both sides
of the glass to come together,
meeting where they speak
a language only
newborns and poets
know.

At eighty-six if you close your eyes
there is always
the chance you might
lurch to the side,
connect with
the wrong piece of furniture
and fall.

It's about answering the moment
with resistance,
risking the act or gift,
deciding there is nothing
more eloquent than the thrill
of giving yourself
to creativity.

In a few days I will contemplate
my mirror image
and surroundings
with eyes wide open,
memory dancing in every cell
and aiming
for eighty-seven.

Ode to Typography

For Rafael Mondragón.

*"Writing begins with the making of footprints,
the leaving of signs. Like speaking, it is a perfectly
natural act which humans have carried to complex
extremes. The typographer's task has always been to
add a somewhat unnatural edge, a protective shell of
artificial order, to the power of the writing hand. The
tools have altered over the centuries, and the exact
degree of unnaturalness desired has varied from place
to place and time to time, but the character of the
essential transformation between manuscript and type
has scarcely changed.*

"Instinct... is largely memory in disguise."

—Robert Bringhurst*

They knew about form and content,
those designers of type
with their modulated strokes, variable axes
and lachrymal terminals.
With or without serifs: medieval, gothic,
baroque, renaissance, classic or postmodern,
they created letters with memories
and strong backbones
ready to make a home for words.

Their font styles shouted or whispered,
sometimes laughed out loud
or sang harmony to a melody
that pressed against the heart
with the strength of forever conviction.
Dangerous secrets fail to thrive
in lettering that knows its place
but will also cross
restrictive lines.

And then there are the innocent secrets
inviting us to games of fantasy.
They may be hiding in plain sight
or require some knowledge of the journey
to reveal themselves,
take us on a passage of discovery
through the words we believe
issue without echo
in our minds.

Font designers were men of rules, and most
were men. I found only a woman or two
among the legion of names.
But their rules extended only as far
as rationale would take them.
These were artists of quiet passion
and balance, and the foundries rang
with the sound of metal bent over anvils
where imagination left its print.

The Elements of Typographic Style, pages 18 and 144.

In Athens and Rome, the modulated stroke
and bilateral serif were symbols
of empire, Sans Serif's
unmodulated forms
spoke for people's resistance
to autocratic rule, cultural souvenirs
of bright periods in human history
when chains were broken
to forge the letters that invite us in.

History told by those who made it
instead of the conquering hero
demands an austere letter,
simple font to give it weight.
A poem written in minor key
may benefit from the mystery
of shapes reminiscent
of an ancient script, unreadable
by anyone alive today.

Tall letters, chorus of downstrokes
in perfect verticals
aren't millennial trees
reaching for the sky
but tell a story
that will take your breath away.
It is the forest and also the trees
speaking through and around
our words.

Less is more when deciding
the aperture of a c or m,
circumference of an o
or how a y drags its injured leg.
Superfluous tangles or twists
may enhance moments of doubt
but steady equilibrium endures
when dignity's pride
is at stake.

In perfect reach, a letter may lean
a degree or two to the right,
another will shift its interior weight
simulating an angle
while you close one eye and imagine
a vessel of old sailing into the wind
and veering off course, a horse
bucking its rider or the Tower of Pisa
resisting gravity all these years.

Analphabetic symbols such as periods,
commas, colons and semicolons,
exclamation points and question marks,
asterisks or dashes of varying widths
differ from typeface to typeface
always trying to maintain the elegance
for which a named design
claims its place in the history
of script.

Italics and bold, Roman and Arabic
pull me from sleep
with a mood to meet the day.
I am Jerónimo Antonio Gil in Mexico City
cutting an Otomí language font in 1785
or Carol Twombly mid-twentieth-century New York,
lone woman among men
creating tilting faces with names
like Lithos, Charlemagne, Nueva, Viva.

In this age of little yellow smiley faces,
pulsing hearts and other emoticons,
Baskerville, Bodoni, Caslon,
Electra, Garamond, Helvetica, Palatino,
Futura and all their kind
are the calm before the storm.
Patience is their virtue,
risk their alter ego, a place
where critical thought stops and waves.

We have gone from chiseled stone
to forged alloy, from handset
to linotype, then photographic methods
and the digital techniques we use today,
each vying for cost-effective labor ease
while maintaining the elegance
of its noble history,
all based on the human body:
eye, hand, and forearm.

This is an artform unique to our species,
the historian tells us, *dogs and ants*
read and write by more chemical means.
Scribes, artists, scholars, calligraphers,
architects, typographers, astronomers,
mathematicians, engravers, poets and printers
have all given us this lettered history
responding to the eager mind
and fingertips of those who see in darkness.

We are talking about pica, not pixels,
breathing the shape of letters,
a history of type that is a map
of writing we explore on foot
that we may touch the space
each letter claims and the distance
in between: the sculptural image
giving form to our meaning
and content to our form.

Bookends

My life gasps between swimming
through the birth canal
and out from between my mother's thighs
to a moment yet to come
when all the lights
will go out, all sound
turn to silence.

Smaller bookends stand watch
at repeated transitions,
marking the first and last hours
in days that follow each other
like frames in a film where color
teases black and white as it spars
with memory.

I wake energized by morning's
prospects, its taunts
and possibilities,
the light and shadow it will cast
upon my aging body
moving through time.
I am eager and alert.

I tread more slowly
than in those years
now braided into the weave
of a half-obscured past,
years when action
counted for more
than questions.

Daybreak and dusk are bookends
focused on this single segment
of a life already stretched
to contain mirrors
reflecting mirrors
like a string of lights
circling an unfamiliar bay.

Excited because my days
are shorter,
my nights more likely
to tempt a greater fate,
I know a final oblivion
watches now from sidelines
closing in.

Whatever it is I will do this day
engages me fully,
gathers me in its embrace
and in its stranglehold,
promises to lead me
to places I may
yet explore.

When I tell each day goodnight
and settle beside the woman
I've loved these many years,
I am wary of dreams
but grateful for sleep, content
when outsized rhythms
lure me away.

I wander the margins
and see the hungry,
those broken by hate
or dragged from place to place.
I would bring them
in from the cold
if I could.

Still, my grateful muscle
embraces this gift
I'm fortunate to hold, lifts me
on the wings of optimism
as I walk a trail
I cede to those
yet unborn.

Footprints

Again, for Raul Zurita.

I am writing these words I want readers
to understand
are about my final days.

There's no indication my end is imminent
but at eighty-six
no guess can take a chance.

Searching for new blooms, I cast out the weeds
and water earth
as parched and dry as failing skin.

Remembering where I stumbled and fell,
glimmers of hope
sprout wings on a landscape of witness.

Writing about the end before arriving at the end
is like remembering
a color photograph in black and white.

You created a glyph etched in Atacama sand
and made of words one can only view
from the sky.

Mine is the small story of a woman hounded
by gender and place
where risk came down on survival's side.

I implore them: stop talking now, listen
in silence to where I am going,
no destination assured.

Trust my memory, what I have seen and felt,
footprints left to be discovered
when life passes this way again.

The Hole in Your Calendar

For Barrett.

Your calendar of important dates,
sad ones and joyous, hovers
beyond that page where eraser force
ripped a hole in memory
calculated to weather any storm.

Those twenty minutes of death
are like a coat hanger
without your old jean jacket
worn by living,
familiar to your skin.

A space where memory has
no foothold. No matter
how hard it tries
it cannot catch up with itself
or rock you back to sleep.

And sleep itself is at risk, you are
only in sync with yourself
when you can hear the steady beat
of your ancient drum
rising this side of emptiness.

Emptiness always corrodes
but when you are
emptied of self you must
guard your limbs and feed your mind
a soil-rich balm.

Newborn once more, you carry
a lifetime of loving,
recognition and escape.
Then milepost zero surprises you
at the trail's edge.

It's those missing minutes, precisely twenty,
that invade your dreams
without invitation, those questions
whose answers are writ
in disappearing ink.

Returning from temporary death
risk repeats itself like minutes
that keep sounding
beyond the finish line, an itch
you cannot scratch.

New life may take your hand
but loss continues
to whisper and call,
telling you stories in a language
you struggle to learn.

You must make peace with
the abyss,
that time when you weren't
leaving you trembling
in present tense.

Echo is your worthy opponent now.
It may threaten to appear
when you least expect its vibrations
to trouble the thinnest membrane
or nestle easily in your palm.

Dubious Gifts

For Leandro Katz.

Animal noises live within us even as Disney
replaces them with voiceover cackles,
erasing nature's memory, playing
for an audience of millions.

Our sons and brothers come with the dubious gift
of *want* translated ritualistically as *need*
or *demand.* We try to help them see the danger
even as they force entry in our flesh.

And we, so often called the weaker sex, are also born
owing a debt that can't be paid except by traveling
obstacle courses strewn with body parts
in the rain-soaked earth of killing fields.

We used to believe only in *us and them,* a concept
we applied to trust, the art of bullying
or the win we accrue by stealing another's water,
tilling another's field.

Defining sex or gender by traditional binary rules
puts freedom off limits or confines it to a zoo
where the mother lion sings a story of vast savannah
to its bewildered young.

In our youth we thought we could subvert those strictures
by ingesting entheogens: Mexican mushroom,
bitter peyote button, or drink. We were left
        with the filmstrip
flapping on a projector crowing to the void.

With age it's memory we harness to perform
        the whole script
in lives where poetry is our language,
landscape our imagination, and justice the only
rule we care to keep.

The Business of Dying

When I'm engaged with the business of dying
I hope the words *I love you*
will be warm hands seeing me off.

I want to die with dignity, my broken body
not getting in the way
of its moment of truth.

To die in the spirit I've lived, no false
prayers to a god I've never
known or rituals not of my making.

As death takes hold, I ask respect for what
I believe, no last-minute proselytizing
or Hail Mary conversion.

Morphine for discomfort, silence as a cradle
for my final thoughts, water soothing
the thirst on my tongue.

No more fear or grief, regret for what I did
or didn't do, those vast empty spaces
filled with what ifs, meaningless excuses.

You and you and you know who you are:
please sit beside me if you can
or think of me as I leave.

As gravity comes undone and I abandon
curiosity past and present,
I am another's memory now.

Not Even the Cheetah

This race to say it all before the finish line
heats up and I worry there's
no more time for words, the poem
you hear before I open my mouth.

Half tortoise but not half hare, maybe
cheetah: the fastest animal.
At times I outrace myself and at others
notice everything in my path.

I must choose between two cadences,
two directions, an option
that wedges itself between my left cheek
and shoulder

like a violin that asks to be played
by the virtuoso who hides
her panic attacks
beneath her pillow at night.

Not a matter of dueling personalities,
hesitation or days when
everything breaks,
mine is a curious arc.

I want to say it all before my journey
fizzles and breathes its last.
But if I can't, no one will be the wiser,
not even the cheetah.

Acknowledgments

"Ode to Typography" was first released as a bilingual chapbook, Spanish translation by Sandra Toro, in a limited run published by Casa Urraca Press (2021). Other poems were published, either in English or Spanish, in *Casa de las Américas* magazine in Havana, Poets in the Libraries Poetry Anthology in Albuquerque, Moonstone's 2021 Featured Poets Anthology in Philadelphia, and *Protean*. I also want to thank Zach Hively for once again curating my poetry so thoughtfully.

Margaret Randall (b. New York, 1936) is a poet, essayist, oral historian, translator, photographer, and social activist. She lived in Latin America for twenty-three years (in Mexico, Cuba, and Nicaragua). From 1962 to 1969, she and Mexican poet Sergio Mondragón co-edited *El corno emplumado / The Plumed Horn*, a bilingual literary quarterly that published some of the best new literature and art of the sixties. She is the author of more than two hundred books.

When she came home in 1984, the government ordered her deported because it found some of her writing to be "against the good order and happiness of the United States." With the support of many writers and others, she won her case in 1989. Throughout

the late 1980s and early 1990s, she taught at several universities, most often Trinity College in Hartford, Connecticut.

She has also devoted herself to translation, producing *When Rains Become Floods* by Lurgio Galván Sánchez, *You Can Cross the Massacre on Foot* by Freddy Prestol Castillo, *Voices from the Center of the World: Contemporary Poets of Ecuador*, and *Only the Road / Solo el camino*, an anthology of eight decades of Cuban poetry. Red Mountain Press in Santa Fe and The Operating System in Brooklyn have brought out her translations of individual Cuban poets. And she rediscovered the poetry of Rita Valdivia, a young combatant in Che Guevara's rebel army, and made it available to an English readership. Randall received the 2017 Medalla al Mérito Literario, awarded by Literatura en el Bravo in Ciudad Juárez, Mexico.

More recent honors received by Margaret include the Poet of Two Hemispheres prize, given by Poesía en Paralelo Cero, Quito, Ecuador, and the Haydée Santamaría Medal, awarded by Casa de las Américas, Cuba, both in 2019. That same year, the University of New Mexico gave her an Honorary Doctorate in Letters. In 2020, AWP named her the year's recipient of its George Garrett Award, and she was honored with the 2019-2020 Paulo Freire Democratic Project Award by Chapman University's Donna Ford Attallah College of Education.

Margaret lives in Albuquerque with her partner (now wife) of more than thirty-six years, the visual artist Barbara Byers, and travels extensively to read, lecture, and teach. You can learn more at her website, margaretrandall.org.

Casa Urraca Press

Casa Urraca Press publishes creative nonfiction, poetry, photography, and other works by authors we believe in. New Mexico and the US Southwest are rich in creative and literary talent, and the rest of the world deserves to experience our perspectives. So we champion books that belong in the conversation—books with the power, compassion, and variety to bring very different people closer together.

We are proudly centered in the high desert somewhere near Abiquiu, New Mexico. Visit us at casaurracapress.com for exquisite editions of our books and to register for workshops with our authors.